For further information, contact:
Tumblehome, Inc.
201 Newbury St, Suite 201
Boston, MA 02116
https://tumblehomebooks.org/

Library of Congress Control Number: 2019955096
ISBN 13: 978-1-943431-52-6
ISBN 10: 1-943431-52-3

Coppens, Katie
Geometry Is As Easy As Pie / Katie Coppens - 1st ed

Design: Yu-Yi Ling

Printed in Taiwan
10 9 8 7 6 5 4 3 2 1

TUMBLEHOME

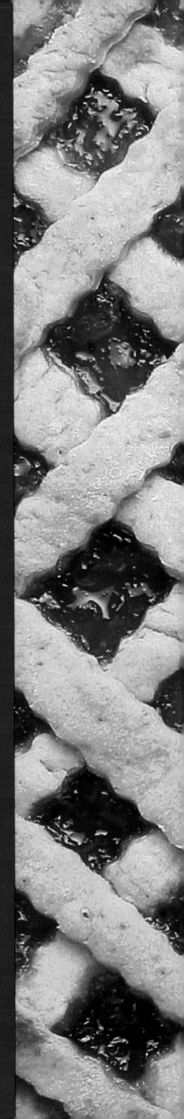

GEOMETRY IS AS EASY AS PIE

KATIE COPPENS

CONTENTS

GEOMETRY

What Do Geometry And Pie Have In Common?

WHAT IS GEOMETRY?

Geometry is the study of shapes and their properties. Concepts in geometry include learning about symmetry, angles, geometric figures, and much more.

Words in math can often be broken down into Greek or Latin root words to help understand their meaning. Geometry is a Greek word that means *earth measuring*. Many terms in geometry are Greek because much of our understanding of geometry came from ancient Greece.

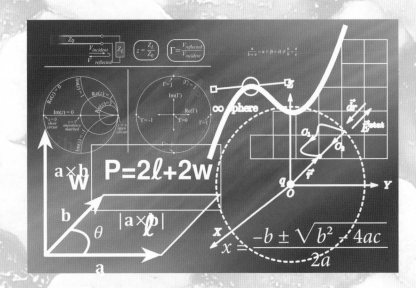

HOW DOES GEOMETRY RELATE TO PIE?

Pie is a delicious food with a sweet or savory filling that is surrounded by a crust. Pie comes in various shapes and has its own unique properties, many of which relate to geometry. Throughout this book, many aspects of pie, ranging from the design of the crust to the angles of how a pie is cut, will serve as a model to help you better understand geometry. You will also discover delicious pie recipes to enhance your geometric thinking and your appetite!

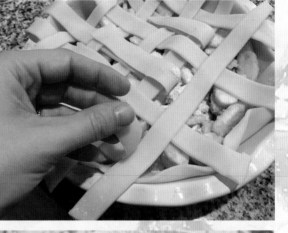

WHAT ARE GEOMETRIC FORMULAS?

Geometric formulas show how concepts are related in a kind of code. Letters are used to symbolize these concepts. For example, the diameter of a circle is two times its radius. If we say d stands for diameter and r stands for the radius, we can write the concept as d = 2r. These formulas work as a shortcut to help solve problems, but it is important to know the mathematical thinking behind formulas.

$$d = 2r$$

HOW DO GEOMETRIC FORMULAS RELATE TO PIE?

Suppose someone asks you how to make a pie and you just read them a recipe out of this book. Will you really understand pie-making as well as if you'd actually made the pie yourself? In the same way, rather than just memorizing geometric formulas, it's important to work with and understand the mathematical ideas behind the formulas. In this book, the thinking behind mathematical concepts is explained first, before we give you formulas. In the same way, we hope you actually try to make the pies you read about in this book!

Recipe For: Butterscotch Pie

1 cup brown sugar packed
5 Tbls. flour
3 egg yolks
1 can evaporated milk
1/4 cup water
3 Tbls. margarine or butter
1 tsp vanilla extract

Combine brown sugar and flour. Add egg yolks and water and milk beat with electric mixer until creamy.

Cook until thickened. Remove from heat and add margarine and vanilla.

Cool then stir well and pour into 8 inch cooked pie shell. Keep refrigerated. good with whipped cream or cool whip.

Grandma Keipel

SYMMETRY
Making Your Pie Pleasing To The Eye!

WHAT IS SYMMETRY?

Symmetry occurs when a shape or a design has equal parts around an axis point or line. Symmetry is a Greek word that means *same measure*.

1 line of symmetry

2 lines of symmetry

3 lines of symmetry

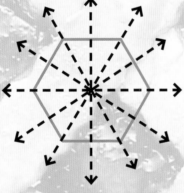

6 lines of symmetry

not symmetrical

HOW DOES SYMMETRY RELATE TO PIE?

There is a theory in baking and cooking that people eat with their eyes first, so it's important to make a pie look appetizing. Whether it be a savory pie, like shepherd's pie, or a sweet apple pie, the top can be made with an artistic design. Such a pie entices your guests with the pie's smell, taste, *and* the way it looks. There are various styles and approaches to creating symmetrical patterns on pie crusts.

WHAT IS REFLECTIONAL SYMMETRY?

Reflectional symmetry occurs when a line of symmetry can be drawn through the middle of a shape or design. What's on one side of that line is an exact mirror image of what's on the other side.

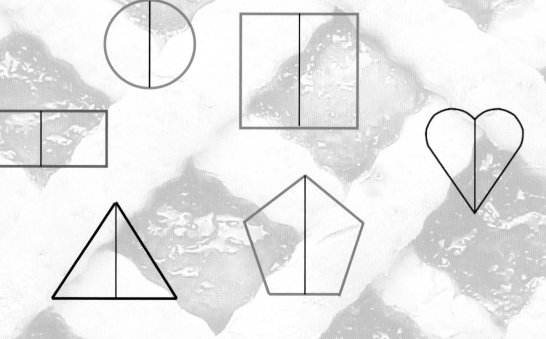

HOW DOES REFLECTIONAL SYMMETRY RELATE TO PIE?

Reflectional symmetry is one of the most common forms of symmetry when creating a pie's design. In the picture to the right of the pie with a butterfly in the center, a knife cutting the pie in half represents the line of symmetry. When the knife cuts the pie, the two halves of the pie will look like mirror images.

WHAT IS ROTATIONAL SYMMETRY?

If you can rotate a shape or design around a center point and find that the shape looks the same after various degrees of rotation, the shape has rotational symmetry. For example, both the star and the butterfly shown below have one vertical axis of reflectional symmetry, but only the star has rotational symmetry. The star looks like a star before turning a full 360 degrees. The butterfly needs to be turned a full 360 degrees before it looks like itself again.

Rotational symmetry

No rotational symmetry

HOW DOES ROTATIONAL SYMMETRY RELATE TO PIE?

Rotational symmetry creates a beautiful artistic balance in how your pie looks. When serving a pie at a table, rotational symmetry causes the pie to look the same to people sitting at different seats around the table. There are tools available that can stamp a design into a pie crust to create rotational symmetry.

WHAT IS ASYMMETRY?

Asymmetry is a lack of symmetry. When the prefix *a* is added in front of a word it means *the opposite* of the word, or *not*. No matter what axis you draw, something that is asymmetrical does not have equal parts on both sides of the axis point.

symmetric

asymmetric

HOW DOES ASYMMETRY RELATE TO PIE?

In pies with asymmetrical designs, not all pieces will look the same. Pies can be slightly asymmetric or have a purposefully random approach to the crust's design. Asymmetrical pies can also be very pleasing to the eye and appetite.

SUPER SIMPLE SYMMETRICAL PUMPKIN PIE

1 package of prepared, refrigerated pie dough (with two pie crusts)

1 can (15 ounces) of pumpkin pie filling | 2 eggs

1 can of sweetened condensed milk | 1 teaspoon of ground cinnamon

½ teaspoon of ginger | ½ teaspoon of nutmeg

Cooking spray

1. Preheat oven to 425 degrees Fahrenheit.

2. In a mixing bowl, crack the eggs and whisk together all ingredients, except for the crusts and cooking spray.

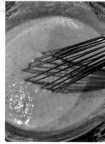

3. Spray the bottom and sides of the pie pan with cooking spray. Lay one of the crusts down over the pie pan. *Try to have the part of the bottom crust that is visible be pushed in with the same approach all the way around; this is called crimping the crust.*

4. Pour mixture from the bowl onto the crust.

5. Bake at 425 degrees for 15 minutes.

6. Roll out the other pie crust onto a counter or cutting board (you may want to put a little flour on the cutting board first to prevent sticking). Using one cookie cutter, cut out eight pieces of that cookie-cutter shape from the pie crust. Spray a cookie sheet with cooking spray and put the cutouts on a cookie sheet.

7. After the pie cooks for 15 minutes at 425 degrees, reduce the heat to 350 degrees and continue to cook the pie for 35 more minutes.

8. While the pie is baking, put the cookie sheet in the oven and cook the cutouts for about 10 minutes or until the cutouts are light brown on the edges.

The length of time will depend on the size of the cutouts. When done, remove the cutouts and continue to cook the pie.

9. Remove the pie from the oven. After the pie is warm, but not hot, find the center of the pie and mark it with a slight indent by a knife or a toothpick. *This will serve as the axis point that all the cutout pieces will revolve around.*

10. Put one of the cutouts below the axis point, put the next above the axis point, *like a mirror reflection.* Using an oven mitt, turn the pie 90-degrees and repeat, so you now have four cutouts placed.

11. Place the remaining cutouts evenly spaced between each of the cutouts that you put down. *This creates rotational symmetry.*

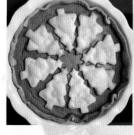

12. When you cut the pie try to cut it into eight equal sized pieces. *This will create eight symmetrical pieces of pie.*

TESSELLATIONS
Can You Tile A Pie?

WHAT IS A TESSELLATION?

A tessellation is a repeating pattern of a shape or design that leaves no gaps or overlaps. This is also called tiling. Tessellate is a Latin word that comes from *tessella*, which means *small square*.

HOW DO TESSELLATIONS RELATE TO PIE?

A tessellation can create the "wow" factor on a pie crust. Certain polygons, like squares, rectangles, and regular hexagons, tessellate easily. More complex shapes can also tessellate. Using a cookie cutter can help to create a uniform design that tessellates.

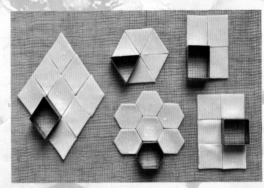

A lattice pastry cutting tool like the one to the right puts cuts in the dough, then you gently pull the dough apart to create gaps that have a tiling effect.

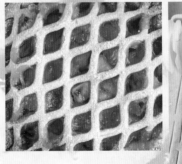

4 red potatoes (peeled and cut into pieces)

1 teaspoon salt

1 teaspoon ground cumin

½ teaspoon of chili powder

3 tablespoons of water

Cooking spray

1 cup of frozen green peas

1 teaspoon garam masala

1 teaspoon ginger powder

3 tablespoons of all purpose flour

20 square egg roll wrappers

Optional additional fillings (cooked carrots, cooked ground turkey, diced jalapeno)

1. Boil the potatoes for 12-14 minutes (until fully cooked).

2. Boil green peas for 3 minutes.

3. Put the potatoes in a mixing bowl and mash them; they should have a chunky, mashed texture.

4. Mix salt, garam masala, cumin, ginger powder, and peas in the bowl with the potatoes and mash.

5. In a separate small bowl mix flour and water to make a paste-like texture.

6. Preheat the oven to 350 degrees Fahrenheit.

7. Fold the square egg roll wrapper in half, then cut it along that line. *The square wrapper will now be two equal-sized rectangles.*

8. Wash your hands, then dip your finger into the flour-water mixture and outline the outside of the wrapper in the shape of a rectangle.

9. Put a spoonful of the mixture on the bottom left corner of the wrapper.

10. Lead with the bottom left corner and fold the wrapper up toward the right side of the rectangle wrapper. Press the edge of the wrappers together, creating an envelope for

the filling that is in the shape of a *triangle. The entire wrapper is now in the shape of a trapezoid.*

11. Fold the triangle with the filling up again. *The wrapper is now in the shape of a square.*

12. Fold the triangle with the filing one more time and press the seam into the wrapper. *You now have a samosa in the shape of an isosceles triangle; two sides of the triangle are the same length.*

13. Repeat this process until all 40 rectangle wrappers are filled.

14. Spray the bottom of a baking sheet with cooking spray. Place the samosas down, then spray the top of each one with more cooking spray.

15. Bake for about 10 minutes or until the edges are lightly browned. Wearing an oven mitt, use tongs or a spatula to flip the samosas over and bake for 4 more minutes.

16. *Because the samosas are made into triangles, they will tessellate easily. To find a tessellating pattern, make sure all triangle points come together and have no gaps. The samosa will be in a triangle with two different types of angles (one 90-degree angle and two 45-degree angles), which can be arranged in different ways to create a tessellating design. Below are some possible designs that show how triangles can tessellate to make the presentation of the hand pies more visually appealing to your guests.*

POLYGONS

Can A Pie Be A Polygon?

WHAT IS A POLYGON?

A polygon is a closed figure made of straight lines that connect to each other without intersecting. Polygon is a Greek word: poly means *many* and gon means *angles*. Regular polygons are when all the angles are equal and all side lengths are equal. Irregular polygons are when side lengths or angles vary in size.

WHAT IS A CLOSED FIGURE?

A closed figure is a two-dimensional figure that has a clear inside and outside.

closed figure   open figure

WHAT IS AN IRREGULAR POLYGON?

An irregular polygon is a specific type of polygon in which not all of the lengths of the lines are equal and/or not all of the angles are equal. When the prefix *ir-* is added in front of a word it means not. For example, this star is an irregular decagon. The lengths of the lines are equal, but the angles are not equal. The figure in the middle is also an irregular decagon because the lines are not all equal and the angles are not equal. The figure on the right is a regular decagon because the lines are equal in measurement and the angles are also equal in measurement.

HOW DO POLYGONS RELATE TO PIE?

Circles are not polygons. Poly means *many* and gons means *angles*; therefore, a circle is not a polygon. However, pies can come in a variety of shapes, not only circles. To the right is an image of a pie pan in the shape of a regular octagon (red pan). The sides of the pan are the same length and the angles where the sides meet are all the same. The square is a regular quadrilateral because the four angles are equal and the side lengths are equal. The rectangular pans represent irregular polygons. Even though the corners of the pan are angles with the same number of degrees, the pan is an irregular polygon because its sides are not all the same length.

CRUSTLESS QUICHE

6 eggs
1 cup shredded cheddar cheese
¾ cup of cut up cherry tomatoes
1 or 2 pinches of ground pepper

1/3 cup of heavy cream
1 cup of cut up baby spinach
1 pinch of salt
Cooking spray

1. Preheat oven to 350 degrees Fahrenheit.

2. Break the eggs into a mixing bowl, then whisk together all ingredients, except for the cooking spray. *With no crust, the melted cheese is what holds this pie together.*

3. Spray the bottom and sides of the pie pan with cooking spray. *The quiche does not have a crust, so the pan represents the closed figure that will give the pie shape.* Pour the ingredients from the bowl into the pan.

4. Bake for 30-35 minutes. Test to see if the quiche is fully cooked by pushing a toothpick into the center of the pie. If it comes out dry, take the quiche out of the oven.

5. Serve warm or cool.

TWO- AND THREE-DIMENSIONAL SHAPES
Can A Pie Be Flat?

WHAT IS A TWO-DIMENSIONAL SHAPE?

A two-dimensional shape is flat; it only has two dimensions. For example, the dimensions of a rectangle are length and width.

HOW DOES A TWO-DIMENSIONAL SHAPE RELATE TO PIE?

A top-view drawing of a pie is two-dimensional; however, nothing involving actual pie that you would eat is two-dimensional. The closest representation of something two-dimensional related to pie is the rolled-out dough for a pie crust, seen from the top. The reason it is not truly two-dimensional is that no matter how flat you try to get the dough, it will also have some height or thickness to it.

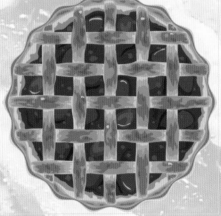

WHAT IS A THREE-DIMENSIONAL SHAPE?

A three-dimensional shape is not flat; it has three dimensions. For example, the dimensions of a rectangular prism are length, width, and height.

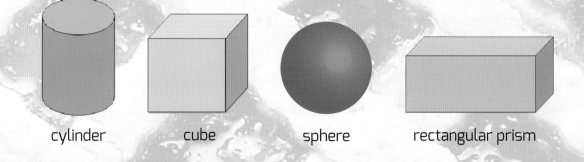

cylinder   cube   sphere   rectangular prism

HOW DOES A THREE-DIMENSIONAL SHAPE RELATE TO PIE?

All pies that you would eat are three-dimensional. The whole pie, a piece of pie, even a tiny crumb of pie have length, width, and height. Some common three-dimensional shapes are the cylinder and the rectangular prism, both of which are common shapes for pie pans.

1 package of prepared, refrigerated pie dough (with two pie crusts)

1/3 cup butter   1/3 cup all-purpose flour

1 teaspoon dried basil   1/4 teaspoon ground pepper

1 ¾ cup reduced-sodium chicken broth   ½ cup milk

2-3 cups of frozen vegetables

2 cups of cut-up cooked chicken (try to cut the pieces into cubes)

1. Preheat oven to 425 degrees Fahrenheit.

2. Over low heat, melt the butter in a large saucepan, then slowly stir in the flour (this is called a roux). Stir in the ground pepper and dried basil.

3. Slowly add the chicken broth and milk. Continue to stir and cook until it starts to bubble.

4. Stir in the chicken and vegetables. Let it cook for three minutes, then remove from heat. *While cooking, pay attention to all the three-dimensional shapes that you see. The peas are spheres, the beans are cylinders, and the pieces of chicken may look like cubes or rectangular prisms.*

5. Spray the bottom and sides of a rectangular cooking dish with cooking spray and place a crust into the dish. If need be, cut and trim the crust to fit the dish. Be sure to push any added seams of the crust together. *This pie will represent a rectangular prism (a 3-D rectangle).*

6. Spoon the chicken and vegetable mixture over the pie crust.

7. Cut out various polygons and place them over the top of the pie. *Some polygons you may include are triangles (right, obtuse, regular), parallelograms, rhombuses, etc.*

8. Brush the top of the pie dough with milk.

9. Put the dish on a baking sheet and bake for 35-40 minutes.

MEASUREMENTS OF A SHAPE

How Many Bites Of Pie Are In Your Pie?

WHAT IS PERIMETER?

Perimeter is the distance around the boundary or border line of a shape. Perimeter is a Greek word in which *peri-* means *around* and *meter* means *measure*. To find the perimeter of a shape, you add up the lengths of all of the sides.

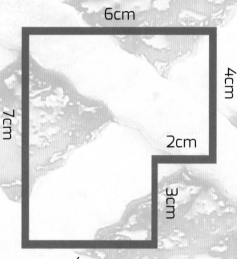

6cm

4cm

7cm

2cm

3cm

4cm

Perimeter= 26cm

6cm + 4cm +2 cm + 3cm +
4cm + 7cm = 26cm

HOW DOES PERIMETER RELATE TO PIE?

Part of what you visualize for a pie is the delicious crust around the pie's outer edge, which is the perimeter of the pie. This flaky, buttery dough is placed in a pie plate or cooking dish to create the shape of the pie. A pizza pie crust in the shape of a rectangle creates a visual representation of the perimeter.

WHAT IS CIRCUMFERENCE?

Circumference is the specific term used for the perimeter of a circle. Circumference is the distance around the boundary or border line of a circle. *Circumference* is a Latin word, in which *circum-* means *around* and *ferre* means to *carry*.

CIRCUMFERENCE

HOW DOES CIRCUMFERENCE RELATE TO PIE?

When a pie is round, the perimeter is called the circumference. Many pies come in a circular shape, whether they are dinner pies, such as pizza or pork pie, or dessert pies, like chocolate mousse pie. There are a variety of round crust types, such as a dough-based crust or a graham cracker crust, but the outer edge all the way around represents the circumference of the pie.

When baking a pie, a tip is to place aluminum foil around the circumference of the raw crust before it is placed in the oven. The aluminum foil prevents the outer crust from getting overcooked. You can also find commercial products that protect the crust in the same way.

WHAT IS DIAMETER?

Diameter is the distance across the center of a circle from one end point to another. To find the diameter you can also find the radius and double it. *Diameter* is a Greek word, in which *dia-* means *across* or *through* and *meter* means *measure*.

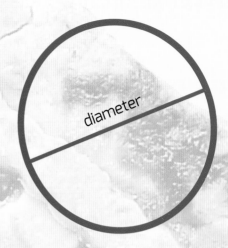

HOW DOES DIAMETER RELATE TO PIE?

When a whole pie is going to be served, the first cut is often made all the way across the center point of the pie, which is the diameter. The cut goes from one side of the crust to the other side of the crust. This causes the pie to be cut in half. A pie is then typically turned and a diameter is cut again, which causes the pie to be cut into four equal quarters. The pie is then turned and cut again along the diameter two more times, causing the pie to be cut into eight equal pieces. Four cuts across the diameter of a pie will create eight equal slices of pie.

WHAT IS PI (Π)?

Pi is the sixteenth letter of the Greek alphabet and is shown by the symbol π. All the way around the outside of a circle is the circumference. When the circumference is divided by the diameter of the circle, it always equals the same amount, regardless of the size of the circle. This amount is pi. Pi is an irrational number, which means it is infinite; it will go on forever. The first 100 decimals of pi are: 3.1415926535 8979323846 2643383279 5028841971 6939937510 5820974944 5923078164 0628620899 8628034825 3421170679... But, pi is often rounded to 3.14.

HOW DOES PI (Π) RELATE TO PIE?

Pi and pie are homophones; they have the same pronunciation, but different spellings and different meanings.

The mathematical term pi only relates to baking if the pie you are making is in the shape of a circle. Regardless of the size of the circle that a pie may be, when the circumference of a pie is divided by the diameter of the pie, it will always equal pi (3.14...).

Try it! If the circumference of a pumpkin pie is almost 30 inches (if you measure it precisely, you will find it's just about 29.845 inches) and the diameter of the pie is 9.5 inches, then you will see that 29.845 divided by 9.5 equals 3.14...

WHAT IS RADIUS?

Radius is the distance from the outer point of a circle to the center of the circle. Radius is a Latin word that means *ray*. A ray is a term in geometry that means a line has an endpoint and extends infinitely (forever) in one direction.

radius

HOW DOES RADIUS RELATE TO PIE?

When it comes to serving only one piece of pie, the first cut is typically from the center point of the pie to the crust. This cut represents the radius of the pie. That cut, like the radius, could be made in any direction to the circumference, as long as it is from the center point of the pie to the crust.

WHAT IS AREA?

Area is the amount of space (in squares) that a two-dimensional shape takes up within the boundaries. One way to measure area is to imagine that something is being divided into lots and lots of small, equal-sized squares. We usually measure smallish areas in square centimeters or square inches. We might measure the floor plan of a house or pie shop in square feet or square meters. If an area is very large, like a town or a national park, we can measure it in square kilometers or square miles.

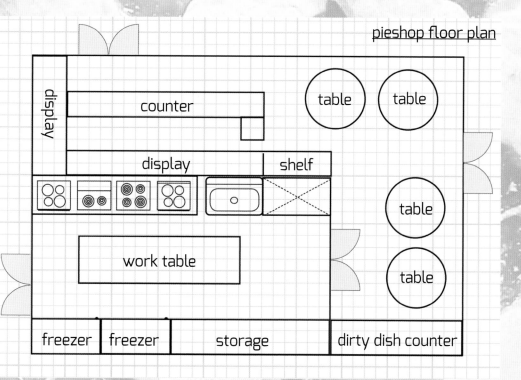

pieshop floor plan

display

counter

table   table

display   shelf

table

work table

table

freezer | freezer | storage | dirty dish counter

There are formulas to help find the area of different two-dimensional shapes. For a rectangle or square, you find the area by multiplying the length times width.

For a circle, you find the area by multiplying the radius times the radius (this is also called squaring it), then multiplying that times pi. The picture of the circle below shows one "**radius square**". Three of these squares would be too few, but four of these radius squares would be larger than the area of the circle. Finding one "radius square" (radius x radius) and multiplying it by pi (remember, pi is about 3.14) will equal the area of the circle.

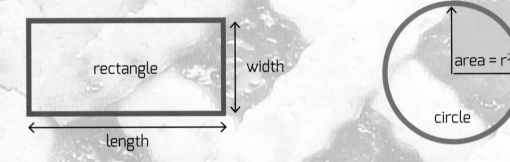

area of rectangle = length x width   circle area = $\pi \times r^2$

HOW DOES AREA RELATE TO PIE?

One of the most important steps when making a pie is thinking about the size of the crust compared to the size of the pan. The area of the crust should be big enough that it can cover the bottom of a pie pan and also go up the sides and hang over by a little bit. This little bit of extra dough is necessary to be able to press the bottom crust and top crust together. If the area of the bottom of the pie crust is not big enough for the pan, it can create a pie with filling that overflows when cooked. If the area of the bottom pie crust is too large for the pan, it can create excess pie crust that needs to be trimmed off. Still, it's better to have too much area for the crust than too little.

If you buy a prepared, refrigerated circular pie crust, it typically has a diameter of 11.5 inches, which means the area of that pie is about 103 square inches. These prepared pie crusts are designed to fit a pie pan with a diameter of eight to ten inches.

WHAT IS VOLUME?

If something is three-dimensional, you can find the volume. Volume is the amount of space something takes up, which is measured in the number of cubes that could fit into the something (cubes are three-dimensional squares). Volume can be measured in cubic centimeters or cubic inches. The volume of something really big, like a lake, can be measured in cubic kilometers or cubic miles. Sometimes volume is measured in a liquid form, by seeing how many milliliters or liters of space something takes up.

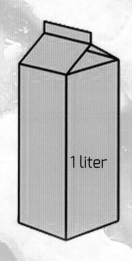

1 liter

There are formulas to help find the volume of different three-dimensional shapes. For a rectangular prism (picture the shape of a tissue box), you find the volume by multiplying the length times the width, then taking that number and multiplying it by the height. Notice that this is the same as finding the area of the base of the prism and then multiplying it by the length of the third dimension (the height).

If something is a cylinder (that is, it has a circular bottom and top, but straight sides) you find the volume by multiplying the area of the circle by the height. To do this, multiply the radius times the radius (one radius square), then multiply that number by pi (3.14) to give you the area of the circle. Then multiply this number by the height.

Notice that volume and area are closely related, but volume is based on three-dimensional shapes, so it includes multiplying by the height, whereas area does not include the height. This is why volume is measured in cubes (three-dimensional) while area is measured in squares (two-dimensional).

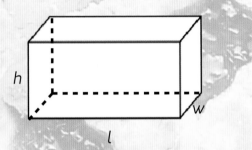

volume of a rectangular prism = lwh

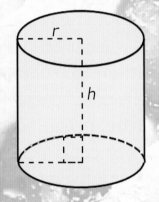

volume of a cylinder = $\pi r^2 h$

HOW DOES VOLUME RELATE TO PIE?

If you imagine yourself cutting a pie into perfect, delicious cubes, the volume of the pie is how many cubes of that pie there would be. If there are 50 one-inch cubes that make up a pie, then the volume of the pie is 50 cubic inches (also called 50 in³). Volume can be found in cubes or it can also be found in milliliters and liters (or if it's really big, kiloliters). If you put a whole pie in a blender and liquify it, you could pour it into a measuring cup and see how many milliliters it contains. Both methods tell you how much three-dimensional space the pie takes up. One method leaves you with perfectly shaped cubes of pie, the other leaves you with a pie shake. Either way, the pie has the same volume and takes up the same amount of space.

WHAT IS SURFACE AREA?

Surface area is the total area of all of the surfaces of something. To find the surface area, you find the area of each side, or surface, then add these together.

6 in

15 in

12 in

Side area = 15 in x 6 in = 90 in²

Side area = 15 in x 6 in = 90 in²

Side area = 12 in x 6 in = 72 in²

Side area = 12 in x 6 in = 72 in²

Side area = 12 in x 15 in = 180 in²

Side area = 12 in x 15 in = 180 in²

Total surface area:
90 in² + 90 in² + 72 in² + 72 in² + 180 in² + 180 in² = 684 in²

HOW DOES SURFACE AREA RELATE TO PIE?

If you are someone who enjoys pie crust, surface area will be one of the most important concepts in this book. If a pie has a crust on the bottom, the sides, and the top, that crust creates a visual representation of the surface area of the pie. By calculating the surface area of a pie, you will know exactly how much crust you could potentially eat!

NO BAKE CHOCOLATE MOUSSE PIE

1 ½ cups of semisweet chocolate chips

1/3 cup of whole milk

2 Tablespoons of butter, cut into quarters

½ teaspoon cinnamon

1 already made graham cracker crust

2 ¾ cup heavy whipping cream (1 cup of this is for the whipped cream topping)

2 cups of mini marshmallows

1 teaspoon vanilla extract

1/8 of a bar of chocolate

1. In a saucepan, add butter, chocolate chips, milk, marshmallows, and cinnamon. Heat on low, stirring constantly, until it all melts together (this can take up to 10 minutes).

2. Pour into a mixing bowl and stir in vanilla. Let cool for about an hour.

3. After the hour has passed, use an electric hand mixer to whip 1 ¾ cups of the heavy whipping cream, until it rises enough that it has stiff peaks. *The process of whipping the cream with a quickly moving electric mixer is increasing the volume of the heavy whipping cream by adding air to the mixture.*

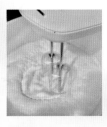

4. Slowly add the whipped cream to the chocolate mixture; stir until it all mixes together. This creates chocolate mousse.

5. Spread the chocolate mousse mixture into the graham cracker crust. *The graham cracker crust covers the area of the bottom and sides of the pie pan. The chocolate mousse mixture is now going to cover most of the surface area of the graham cracker crust, leaving only the upper circumference*

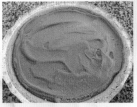

of the crust exposed. The chocolate mousse is also taking up most of the volume of the pie pan.

6. Chill for at least 3 hours or as long as overnight.

7. Use an electric hand mixer to whip 1 cup of the heavy whipping cream and slowly add 2 tablespoons of sugar to the cream. Mix until it rises enough to have stiff peaks.

8. Evenly spoon on and spread the whipped cream over the chocolate mousse. *As you spread the whipped cream over the chocolate mouse, think about how you are covering the surface area of the mousse.*

9. Either cut the chocolate bar into small pieces or use a grater. *Whether you cut or grate the chocolate, the overall volume of the chocolate will be the same as when it was in bar form. However, by making it into smaller pieces, you are increasing the total amount of surface area of the chocolate.*

10. Cover the area of the whipped cream with as much chocolate as you think people would enjoy. Then cut and serve.

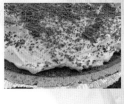

PARALLEL AND PERPENDICULAR LINES

At Last It's Time For Lattice!

WHAT ARE PARALLEL LINES?

Parallel lines are two lines that will never touch because they are always the same distance apart. Parallel is a Greek word, in which *para-* means *beside* and *allelon* means *of one another*.

HOW DO PARALLEL LINES RELATE TO PIE?

A great way to make your pie fancier is to learn how to do a properly constructed lattice top crust. You can create a lattice top on a pie by intertwining strips of the crust in a woven pattern. The woven pattern shows both parallel and perpendicular lines. When making the lattice of a pie, you first cut the dough into parallel strips. Depending on the pattern, the strips of dough can be the same or different widths. The next step in creating a lattice top is to lay all the dough strips down, evenly spaced, with or without a little bit of the filling of the pie showing between them. To keep the lattice looking consistent, all of the dough strips should be parallel lines. If the dough strips are not parallel, the weaving pattern will be off and the lattice can look uneven.

WHAT ARE PERPENDICULAR LINES?

Perpendicular lines are lines that meet at a 90-degree (or right) angle. Perpendicular is a Latin word that means *vertical, as a plumb line*. In ancient times, builders used a plumb line (a piece of lead, or *plumbum*, hanging from a string) to ensure walls were straight.

HOW DO PERPENDICULAR LINES RELATE TO PIE?

Much as a plumb line was used to build walls properly, it is also important that you weave your lattice top correctly to ensure proper construction. After placing the parallel pieces of dough down, the next step of a lattice pie top is to weave in perpendicular strips of dough. The simplest way to do this is to pull back every other strip of parallel dough, then place a perpendicular strip of dough down flat. Then return the parallel strips to the original position, so dough is now weaved over and under. Next, pull back every other parallel dough strip and again place a dough strip down that is perpendicular to the parallel ones. Continue this weaving pattern until it creates a lattice top for the pie. Regardless of how thick or thin the strips of dough are, if they are evenly spaced apart, this represents parallel and perpendicular lines.

It is worth taking the time to make any adjustments so the dough strips are perpendicular because once the crust is baked, they cannot be moved.

PARALLEL AND PERPENDICULAR LATTICE APPLE PIE

1 package of prepared, refrigerated pie dough (with two pie crusts)

½ cup sugar   ½ cup all-purpose flour

1 teaspoon cinnamon   ½ teaspoon cornstarch

1 tablespoon lemon juice   1 tablespoon butter

1 tablespoon milk   Cooking spray

5 large apples peeled and thinly sliced

1. Preheat oven to 425 degrees Fahrenheit.

2. Mix dry ingredients (sugar, flour, and cinnamon) in a large bowl.

3. Peel apples and cut into thin, even slices. *As you peel, think about how the skin of the apple represents the surface area of the apple.* Add half the lemon juice to a bowl, add apple slices to the bowl, then add the rest of the lemon juice and stir.

4. Add apples to the bowl of dry ingredients and mix together.

5. Spray the bottom and sides of a pie plate with cooking spray and put down one unbaked pie dough crust.

6. Add the apple mixture over the dough and spread it out evenly.

7. Dot the top of the pie with small cut-up pieces of butter.

8. Cut the remaining prepared crust into even strips. *Using a ruler and a rolling pizza cutter to cut the dough can help keep the strips even. As you cut, notice how these strips are making parallel lines.*

9. Evenly space strips across the top of the pie. *These strips of dough should look like parallel lines.*

10. Fold up every other strip and place down another strip of dough going in the other direction. *These strips of dough should look like perpendicular lines.* Unfold the dough strips so they are flat. Fold up every other dough strip starting with the next parallel line. Continue this weaving pattern until the entire top of the pie makes a lattice. *These strips of dough should make parallel and perpendicular lines.*

11. Trim off the excess dough that is hanging off the sides of the pie plate. Gently squeeze the lattice top to the crust, sealing them together. This is called crimping the crust.

12. Brush the top of the pie dough with milk.

13. Bake for 30 minutes.

14. Cut and serve.

ANGLES
Finally, We Get To Serve And Eat The Pie!

WHAT IS AN ANGLE?

An angle is created when two lines or rays connect. Angles are measured in degrees; the smaller the number of degrees, the smaller the angle.

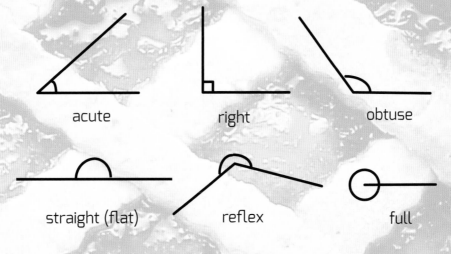

acute   right   obtuse

straight (flat)   reflex   full

HOW DOES AN ANGLE RELATE TO PIE?

Now that you have baked the pie, it's time to eat it! This means it's also time to cut the pie, for which you need to understand angles. There are two cut lines that come together to create a piece of pie. The size of a piece of pie depends on how much pie someone intends to eat. The bigger the piece of pie, the bigger the angle measurement.

WHAT IS A FULL ANGLE?

A full angle, which can also be called a round angle, is exactly 360 degrees. A full angle is a complete circle.

360°

HOW DOES A FULL ANGLE RELATE TO PIE?

Before a pie is served, it represents a full angle of a 360-degree circle. Once the pie is gone, there are 0 degrees of pie left.

WHAT IS A RIGHT ANGLE?

There are 360 degrees in a circle. A right angle is a 90-degree angle or one fourth of a full circle. A square has four corners, all of which have 90-degree angles. A right angle is often shown with a symbol that looks like a square.

90°

HOW DOES A RIGHT ANGLE RELATE TO PIE?

Sometimes, the pie you make is so appetizing, with its beautifully designed crust and delightful smell, that people insist on having equal-sized pieces. To cut a pie into eight even pieces, it is best to first cut the pie in half along the diameter, then turn it and cut it in half again along the diameter. This creates four large pieces that, if cut evenly, all have 90-degree angles. If you cut each piece in half again, you will create eight even pieces, all of which are half of 90 degrees, which is 45 degrees. By cutting the pieces evenly, you give everyone the same amount of your delicious pie to enjoy!

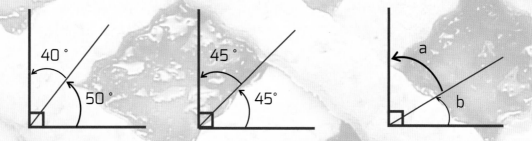

WHAT IS A COMPLEMENTARY ANGLE?

Complementary angles are two angles that add up to equal 90 degrees. Both of these angles are acute angles.

HOW DO COMPLEMENTARY ANGLES RELATE TO PIE?

To increase the odds of complementary pie pieces, it helps to first cut the pie into four 90-degree angles, then ask your guests what size piece they'd like. One guest may want a small piece, like one that is 20 degrees, and another guest may want a larger piece. You could give that guest the 70-degree piece of pie. Those two pieces add up to 90 degrees and are complementary angles. Or one guest may start thinking they want a 45-degree piece, but after tasting it decide they want more. You could give them the remaining 45-degree-angle piece. The two angles that they ate totaled 90 degrees, meaning they were complementary angles. A good way to remember the meaning of complementary angles is that it is a compliment to the chef if someone asks for a second piece of pie to make a total of 90 degrees, since this is a quarter of the whole pie!

WHAT IS AN ACUTE ANGLE?

An acute angle measures more than 0 degrees and less than 90 degrees. Acute is a Latin word that means *sharp, pointed.*

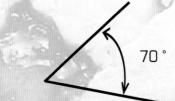

12°

70°

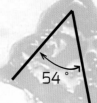

54°

HOW DOES AN ACUTE ANGLE RELATE TO PIE?

The size of the piece of pie someone gets is often determined by how hungry they are or how many people are sharing the pie. Typically, a slice of pie is

an acute angle, which is smaller than a quarter of the pie (less than 90 degrees). If someone asks for a tiny sliver of pie, like one that is 1 to 20 degrees, they are just looking for a taste of the pie. If they are really hungry, they may ask for an acute piece of pie that is between 60 and 89 degrees.

WHAT IS AN OBTUSE ANGLE?

An obtuse angle is wider than 90 degrees and less than 180 degrees. Obtuse is a Latin word that means *dull, blunt.*

116 °   94 °   168 °

HOW DOES AN OBTUSE ANGLE RELATE TO PIE?

You know your guests are excited about the pie when they ask for an obtuse piece of pie! That is more than a quarter of a pie! Anything from a 91-degree angled piece of pie all the way to a 179-degree angle piece of pie will be obtuse. Even a 90.000001-degree piece of pie and a 179.999999-degree angle of pie are obtuse. Someone asking for an obtuse piece of pie shows how nice a job you did making the pie, but you may want to limit how large the obtuse angle can be so that plenty of pie remains for the rest of your guests.

WHAT IS A STRAIGHT ANGLE?

A straight angle is an angle that is exactly 180 degrees. A straight angle looks like a straight line and is also called a flat angle.

180 °

HOW DOES A STRAIGHT ANGLE RELATE TO PIE?

Some grocery stores and bakeries sell pies that are cut in half, which creates a visual of a straight angle. These half pies actually have their own unique packaging, which is a semi-circle.

WHAT ARE SUPPLEMENTARY ANGLES?

Supplementary angles are two angles that add up to equal 180 degrees. Unless they are both right angles, one supplementary angle will end up being acute and the other will end up being obtuse.

120 °   60 °

a + b = 180

a   b

supplementary angles

HOW DO SUPPLEMENTARY ANGLES RELATE TO PIE?

If you purchase a half a pie or if you have a half of a pie left, the first cut that you make will create two supplementary angles. If one angle is 145 degrees and the other is 35 degrees, they are supplementary angles. If one angle is 95 degrees and the other piece's angle is 85 degrees, they are supplementary angles. If two pieces are cut that are equal, at 90 degrees, they are also supplementary angles. Any two pieces whose angles equal 180 degrees are supplementary.

WHAT IS A REFLEX ANGLE?

A reflex angle is bigger than 180 degrees and less than 360 degrees.

244°   255°   192°

HOW DOES A REFLEX ANGLE RELATE TO PIE?

When you cut a piece of pie, you can look at the pie in two ways, the angle of the piece and the angle of what remains. When a piece of pie is cut, it leaves the rest of the pie, which can be visualized as a reflex angle. The bigger the piece of pie taken out, the smaller the reflex angle is. For example, if a piece of pie is 20 degrees, then the pie still remaining in the pan is a reflex angle of 340 degrees.

To have pie humor with someone, you could ask them to cut a 45-degree piece of pie. But instead of taking that piece of pie, you could say that you prefer reflex angles over acute angles as you reach for the 315 degrees of remaining pie.

Which piece will you take?

WHAT IS A CONGRUENT ANGLE?

Congruent angles have the same angle measurement. Congruent is a Latin word that means *to agree* or *to come together*.

110 °

110 °

48 °

48 °

HOW DO CONGRUENT ANGLES RELATE TO PIE?

Some guests will be upset if everybody's piece of pie is not exactly the same size. If you ever struggle in cutting your piece pieces equally, there is a tool that can help you! Here you can see a top view and bottom view of this tool, which cuts a pie into eight equal pieces so that all are congruent and all 45-degree angles.

WHAT IS A VERTICAL ANGLE?

When two lines cross, they create vertical angles, which lie opposite one another. Vertical angles are always equal. Therefore, vertical angles are also congruent angles.

two sets of vertical angles

HOW DO VERTICAL ANGLES RELATE TO PIE?

Imagine there are four people sharing a pie, but they have different levels of hunger. This is where vertical angles can come in really handy! If one cut is made across the diameter of a pie, then you turn the pie, but not at a full 90-degree angle, it will create two pairs of vertical angles. Each pair of vertical angles creates two pieces opposite each other that are the same size (congruent). Of course, creating two cuts that make four 90-degree angles also show vertical angles. In this case all four angles are equal.

WHAT IS AN ADJACENT ANGLE?

Adjacent means "next to." Adjacent angles are angles that have a common vertex and a common side. The vertex is the point where two or more rays or lines meet.

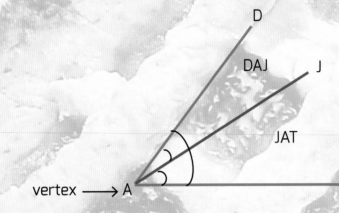

HOW DO ADJACENT ANGLES RELATE TO PIE?

Adjacent angles, or adjacent pieces of pie, share a common cut line and a common vertex.

Crust:
2 cups of all-purpose flour
2/3 cup butter (softened slightly and cut up)
1 teaspoon salt
5-7 tablespoons cold water

Filling:
2 cups of berries (any combination of blueberries, strawberries, raspberries, etc.)
2/3 cup sugar
¾ cup flour
1 Tablespoon cornstarch
Cooking spray
3 mini pie pans with a diameter 3 – 5 inches

1. Preheat oven to 375 degrees Fahrenheit.

2. Put the flour and a pinch of salt in a food processor. With the motor turned off, add a piece of the cut-up butter, then place the top on and (carefully) turn the food processor on. Turn the processor off and repeat the process of adding cut butter chunks one at a time until all of the butter has been mixed in. Do the same process of adding one tablespoon of cold water at a time until the mixture has a dough-like texture that is not wet, but also not so dry that it crumbles apart.

3. Unplug the food processor and remove the dough. Using your hands, press the dough together. *You can either form the dough into one large sphere or smaller spheres for each of the pie pans.* Depending on the size of the pie pans, this recipe is enough for three or four individual pies.

4. Dust your surface and rolling pin with flour. Roll out the dough until it is the thickness that you like.

5. *Measure the diameter and the depth of your mini pie pans to determine how large the bottom*

crust should be. Placing the mini pie pans upside down over the crust can make it easier to cut out the larger circle around them.

6. Spray the bottom of the pie pans with cooking spray and place the crusts down.

7. Now in a mixing bowl make the filling. Larger fruit like strawberries should be cut

into pieces. Combine a total of two cups of berries in a bowl and mix in the sugar, flour, and cornstarch.

8. Place the filling over the bottom crust.

9. With the extra crust, try to make each top crust look unique by using cookie cutters and lattice tops.

10. Bake for 35-40 minutes.

11. *No need to cut these pies; all 360 degrees of the pie are for eating!*

PUTTING IT ALL TOGETHER WITH ONE FINAL PIE

Yum!

To take your apple pie to a whole new level of geometry, you can try to incorporate what you have learned into one stunning pie!

When peeling the skin off of apples for the filling of an apple pie, the skin on the outside of an apple represents the *surface area* of the apples. An apple is close in shape to a sphere. To find the surface area of a sphere you multiply the radius times the radius, then take that number and multiply it by pi (3.14...), then multiply that by number by four. Another way of saying this is surface area= $4\pi r^2$, which is like the apple being covered by four circles with the same radius.

The crust covers the *area* of the bottom and sides of the pie pan.

The lattice top on the pie shows lines that are *parallel*, *perpendicular*, and have *right angles*. The right angles are congruent angles. The lattice also creates a pattern that *tessellates*.

For this pie, a cookie cutter pattern of a leaf is used to decoratively show the *circumference*. Knowing the *diameter* of the pie, the *radius* and the *area* of the pie

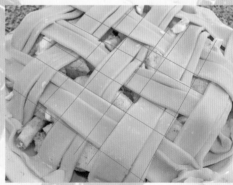

can also be found. This information can also help you determine the *volume* of the pie, which is the number of cubic inches of pie crust and filling that will be eaten.

The cookie cutter pattern can be continued to create a pie that has *rotational symmetry*.

The next step is to ask people what *angle* of a piece (*acute, right, obtuse, or maybe even reflex*) they would like to eat! Or, to make sure there is enough pie to go around, you may want to cut the pie with *congruent angles*.

The final step is to eat and enjoy the pie until there are zero cubic inches of pie left!

ONE MORE PIECE, PLEASE!

Pie-Related Math Problems

1. Can a pie that is made in a rectangular shape have *rotational symmetry*? Can it have *reflectional symmetry*? Explain your thinking.

2. Draw out a crust design of a pie (circular, square, or rectangular) that is *asymmetrical*, but when cut into 8 even-sized pieces, will have exactly 4 pieces that are *symmetrical*.

3. Which of the following cookie cutters could *tesselate* on the top of a pie crust?

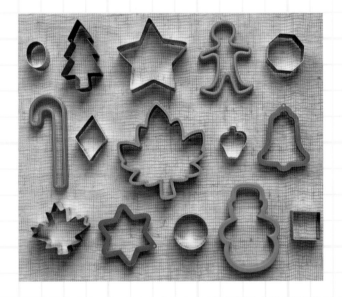

4. Each *interior angle* on a *regular triangle* is 60 degrees. Each interior angle on a regular quadrilateral (a square) is 90 degrees. Each *interior angle* on a regular hexagon is 120 degrees. Observe the *vertex point* where the *angles* come

together for the tessellations made by these *regular polygon* cookie cutters. What do all of the angles add up to at the vertex? Can you come up with a rule for determining if a polygon will be able to *tessellate*?

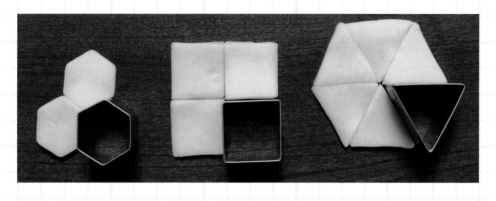

5.   When paired with a square, a regular octagon will tessellate. Is there another combination of regular polygons that will tessellate? Why are they able to tessellate?

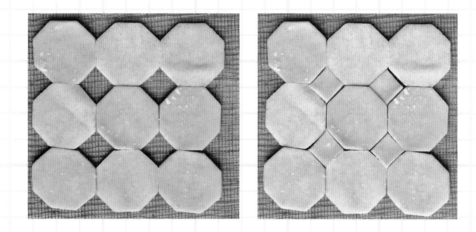

6.   If you are making a pie to serve 10 people equal-sized slices, what shape would you want the pan to be and why? There are lots of possible answers to this question, so explain your thinking.

7.   A *parallelogram* is a polygon with four sides whose opposite sides are parallel and the same length as each other. If you want to make a pie that is the shape of a parallelogram, could you use a rectangular, square, or rhombus-shaped pie pan? Why or why not?

8. If pie dough is first kneaded into the shape of a *sphere*, is it easier to then roll it into a circle, a square, or a rectangle? Why?

9. Create two pie designs (include dimensions) that have the same *volume*, but different *surface areas*. If you were to bake these pies, would they have the same baking time? Why or why not?

10. If one pumpkin pie fills an 8-inch *diameter* round pie pan that is 1 inch deep, and another pumpkin pie fills an 8-inch diameter round pie pan that is 2 inches deep, what is the difference in *volume* of the two pies?

11. How does the *volume* change if instead of filling an 8-inch *diameter* round pie pan that is 2 inches deep, you fill a pie pan with a 9-inch diameter that is 2 inches deep?

12. This is a tool that guides a baker in rolling out dough to a certain *diameter*. If the same amount of dough is rolled to 6 inches, or 9 inches, or 12 inches, find the *circumference* and *area* for each rolled-out crust.

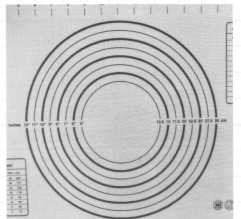

13. Each of the 3 rolled out dough crusts below has a different *diameter*, *circumference*, and *area*, but they all have the same *volume*. Explain how that is possible.

(6 inch diameter)   (9 inch diameter)   (12 inch diameter)

14. A rectangular pie pan has the dimensions of 9 inches by 5 inches by 2 inches and holds exactly 400 blueberries. Would a rectangular pie pan that is 18 inches by 10 inches by 4 inches hold 800 blueberries? Find the *volume* of each pan to explain your thinking.

15. This is a pumpkin pie and a chocolate mousse pie stacked on top of each other (yum!). Without using a ruler and getting dimensions of the pie, what is a method that you could use to find the volume of this stacked pie?

16. If the *circumference* of a pie is 18 inches, using what you know about pi, how can you figure out the diameter of the pie?

17. Suppose you buy a premade circular pie dough that has a diameter of 12 inches, but you need the pie dough to be cut into a square shape for the pan that you are using. Rather than rolling up the dough and forming it into a square, you cut a square out of the circular dough. What is the largest size square that you could cut out of the circular dough?

18. Below are 3 different styles of lattice crusts. Even though they look different, how do all 3 show examples of parallel lines?

19. Do any of the pies above also show *perpendicular* lines?

20. Regardless of the size of pieces cut from a round pie, what do all of the *angles* of pieces always add up to? Why?

21. List every type of *angle* that you can identify in this cut pie.

22. How many geometric concepts could you apply to this one pie?

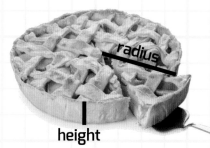

Pie-related math problems that go beyond geometry

23. All pies at a bakery are $15. They have a special that you can buy four pies for a total of $50. How much money does this save you?

24. A dough recipe calls for one and a quarter sticks of butter. If you plan to triple the recipe, how many sticks of butter will you need in all? One stick of butter equals a ½ cup of butter. How many cups of butter does the tripled recipe require?

25. Four friends are sharing a pie. One friend has ¼ of the pie, one friend has 1/3 of the pie, and two friends each have 1/8 of the pie. How much pie is left over?

26. You made one pie, but 3 people want different sized pieces that would lead to the entire pie being eaten. What are three different fractions, each with a numerator of 1, that will equal 1 whole?

$$\frac{1}{} + \frac{1}{} + \frac{1}{} = 1$$

27. If a pie is divided in half, then each of those pieces is divided in half again, then each piece is divided into thirds, how many equal-sized pieces are there?

28. What is the minimum number of cuts you can make to cut a pie into 5 equal pieces? Are there more or fewer cuts to make a pie into 6 equal pieces? Explain.

29. What is the minimum number of cuts to cut a pie into 2 equal pieces? 4 equal pieces? 8 equal pieces? 16 equal pieces? There is a pattern to the number of cuts. Why? Can you predict how many cuts it would take to cut a pie into 72 equal pieces?

30. This is a pie graph that represents people's favorite types of pie out of three choices: blueberry crumb, pecan, or pumpkin pie. Create a pie graph to show what it would look like if 5 out of 10 people's favorite pie is blueberry crumb, 2 out of 10 people's favorite pie is pecan, and 3 out of 10 people's favorite pie is pumpkin pie.

* The answers to the questions can be found at https://tumblehomebooks.org/

JUST DESSERTS
Pie Pictures As Inspiration

glossary

acute angle	a type of angle that is more than 0 degrees and less than 90 degrees
acute triangle	a triangle with each angle measuring less than 90 degrees (acute)
adjacent angles	two angles with a common line (or ray) and a common vertex
angle	the figure formed when two lines intersect or two rays connect
apex	a vertex at the top of a figure, such as at the top of a cone
area	the amount of space (in squares) a two-dimensional shape takes up
asymmetry	when a shape or design does not have symmetry
axis point	a point around which a geometric figure can rotate
circumference	the name for the perimeter of a circle
closed figure	an enclosed shape with no overlapping lines
complementary angles	angles that add up to equal 90 degrees
cone	a 3-D figure with a round base and sides that come together at an apex
congruent angles	angles that are equal in measurement
cube	a 3-D figure with six sides that are squares
cylinder	a 3-D figure with a flat, round bottom/top and straight sides
diameter	the distance straight across a circle, from one point on the circumference through the center point to another point on the circumference.
full angle	(or round angle) a type of angle that measures exactly 360 degrees
geometry	the study of shapes and their properties

interior angle	an angle on the inside of a polygon that is formed where two sides meet
irregular polygon	a type of polygon in which line lengths and/or angles are not equal
isosceles triangle	a triangle that has two sides with equal length and two equal angles
line of symmetry	a line that divides a shape or design into equal parts
obtuse angle	a type of angle that measure more than 90 degrees and less than 180 degrees
obtuse triangle	a triangle with an obtuse angle
open figure	(or a non-closed figure) a figure not enclosed with connecting lines
parallel lines	two or more lines that will never touch
parallelogram	a four-sided polygon with opposite sides that are the same length and parallel to each other
perimeter	the distance around the boundary or border line of a shape
perpendicular lines	lines that meet at a 90-degree (right) angle
pi (or π)	the ratio of a circle's circumference to its diameter
polygon	a closed figure made of straight lines that connect
radius	the distance from the outer point of a circle to the center of a circle
ray	a line with one endpoint and one end that extends forever
rectangular prism	a 3-D figure that has six rectangular sides
reflectional symmetry	mirror symmetry; a property of a figure that shows a mirror image on each side of an imaginary line
reflex angle	a type of angle that measures more than 180 degrees and less than 360 degrees

regular polygon	a specific type of polygon with equal side length and equal angles
rhombus	a parallelogram with four equal sides and opposite angles that are equal in measure
right angle	a type of angle that is exactly 90 degrees
right triangle	a triangle with a right angle
rotational symmetry	when a shape looks the same if you turn it less than 360 degrees
sphere	a 3-D figure that is perfectly round in all directions
straight angle	(or a flat angle) a type of angle that is exactly 180 degrees
supplementary angles	two angles that add up to equal 180 degrees
surface area	the total area of all of the surfaces of something
symmetry	when a shape or design has identical parts reflected across a line or rotated around an axis point
tessellation	a repeating pattern of a shape or design that has no gaps
three-dimensional	(or 3-D) with three dimensions such as length, width, & height
trapezoid	a quadrilateral with at least one set of parallel lines
two-dimensional	(or 2-D) with two dimensions such as length and width
vertex	where two or more rays or lines meet (plural of vertex is vertices)
vertical angles	equal angles made across from each other when two lines cross
volume	the amount of space (cubes) a three-dimensional shape takes up

about the author

Katie Coppens lives in Maine with her husband and two children. She is an award-winning teacher who started her career as a middle school math teacher. She has since taught all subjects in third through sixth grade, and also taught high school biology and English in Tanzania. With any grade or subject, Katie emphasizes the value of creative and critical thinking. Katie has multiple publications, including a teacher's guide for the National Science Teaching Association entitled *Creative Writing in Science: Activities That Inspire, Geology is a Piece of Cake,* and *The Acadia Files* chapter book series. Katie also writes a column for NSTA's Science Scope magazine called "Interdisciplinary Ideas". For more information on her publications, please visit *www.katiecoppens.com*.

acknowledgments

I would like to thank the amazing staff at Tumblehome Books! This whole concept came together when Penny Noyce and I were sitting down together and eating pie. Penny Noyce's editing feedback helped shape the direction and voice of the book. A big thank you to Yu-Yi Ling and Barnas Monteith for creating the book's design and cover.

Thank you to my past and present students who were delighted by the thought of a book similar to *Geology is a Piece of Cake*, but this time involving learning math through the analogy of pie. And thank you to one of my 6th-grade students for suggesting a maroon book cover.

Thank you to my amazing colleagues at Falmouth Middle School who provided feedback on the manuscript; Sally Bennett, Joyce Hebert, Craig Shain, and Mat Holmes. You helped with everything from wordsmithing to testing out the math problems to recommending that I include samosa hand pies. I have so much respect and appreciation for all of you!

Thank you to my husband, Andrew McCullough, for his endless support with everything from posing as a hand model to helping me with rounds and rounds of pie-related dishes. And thank you to my daughters for all the smiles we had while talking about math while eating lots and lots of pie!

photo credits

Mathematical images are done by YuYi Ling, unless noted in credits. The author took over 100 of the photographs printed in this book. All pie-related photographs are by Katie Coppens with the exception of:

Cover (also repeated in the book):
Strawberries rotating over whipped cream: by Kseniia Konakova via Shutterstock (cropped)
Pumpkin pie: from Shutterstock by Elena Veselova (cropped)
Serving cut pie with lattice top: from Shutterstock by Split Second Stock
Three pies together in one pie: by Elena Veselova from Shutterstock (cropped)
Snowflake chocolate pie: Joy's "Crunchy, buttery Crispix crust + peanut butter chocolate ganache + a dusting of powdered sugar = Puppy Chow Pie!", on creative commons via flickr
Flag pie: from Shutterstock by Africa Studio (cropped)
Key lime pie: from Shutterstock by Goskova Tatiana (cropped)
Pie with apples: by DronG via Shutterstock
Symmetrical quiche: by L.A. Foodie, quiche made by chef Jules, on creative commons via flickr
Apple tart spiral- Cropped: by forden via Shutterstock (cropped)

Book content:
p.1 Blue geometry image: by geralt via Pixabay
p.3, 9, 11, 12, 17, 20, 31, 34, 45 Hands making a pie crust: Stolyevych Yuliya via Shutterstock
p.2 Cut cherry pie: by Beckmann's bakery called "Beckmann's Old World Bakery Cherry Pie", on creative commons via flickr
p.5 Apple pie that looks like rose petals: by Mikhaylovskiy via Shutterstock (cropped)
p.6 Orange butterfly: OpenClipart-Vectors via Pixabay
p.10 Winged horse tessellation: by Martin Janecek via Shutterstock
p.10 Wave tessellation: by elfinadesign via Shutterstock
p.10 Peach pie tessellating top (zoomed in): by DronG via Shutterstock (cropped)
p.14 Cut peach/blueberry pie with a pie server resting on the pan: by Denise I Johnson via Shutterstock (cropped)
p.18 Drawing of cherry pie uncut: by freesoulproduction via Shutterstock
p.18 Rolled dough and rolling pin: by Corina Daniela Obertas via Shutterstock
p.19 Cylinder Chicken Pot Pie: by Luisrftc via Shutterstock (cropped)
p.19 Rectangular shepherd's pie (white dish): by gkrphoto via Shutterstock (cropped)
p.21 Rectangular pizza: by Sara Winter via Shutterstock (cropped)
p.22 Pecan pie with a white background: by jesmo5 via Shutterstock
p.27 Pie crust in pan with rolling pin: "pie crust" by Kimberly Vardeman via flickr
p.30 Surface area round pie (chicken pot pie in glass dish): "photo of simple chicken pot pie" by Foodista, on creative commons via flickr
p.30 Surface area square pie (chicken pot pie in glass dish): by farbled via Shutterstock (cropped)
p.33 "vegan cherry pie" by Stephanie from Austin TX, wikimedia commons
p.35 Cut cherry pie with lattice top on green and white napkin: by from my point of view via Shutterstock (cropped)
p.42 Reflex angle strawberry rhubarb pie with fork/knife: by JeniFoto via Shutterstock
p.43 Cherry pie uncut with lattice top- top view: by canbedone via Shutterstock (also used as background image)
p.43 Cherry pie symmetrical cuts with white space in between- top view: by canbedone via Shutterstock
p.44 Lemon meringue pie/tart cut with two pieces in focus: by Alyona Mandrik via Shutterstock
p. 52 Lattice question pie angled lattice (with strawberries):By Pixel-Shot via Shutterstock (cropped)
p.52 Lattice question thick and thin crust and metal pan: by Oksana Mizina via Shutterstock (cropped)
p.52 Lattice question even crust and brown background: by GreenArt via Shutterstock (cropped)
p.53 Cut Pumpkin pie with purple background: by YesPhotographers via Shutterstock (cropped)
p.53 Server under piece of pie with white background: by Pixel-Shot via Shutterstock
p.55 Lattice pie with flowers and yellow tile in back: by Lisa Cardoza Routh via Shutterstock (cropped)
p.55 Flower crust with dollop in the middle: by Natallia Harahliad via Shutterstock (cropped)
p.55 Pumpkin pie with a decorative leaf top: by Anatolii Riepin via Shutterstock (cropped)
p.55 Berry ring on the outside of the crust: by Elena Veselova via Shutterstock (cropped)
p.55 6 small pies with powdered sugar: by Julia Sudnitskaya via Shutterstock (cropped)
p.55 Pecan pie with pecans in round pattern on top: by AlexelLogvinovich via Shutterstock (cropped)
p.55 Roses on the left of lattice crust: by the foodphotographer via Shutterstock (cropped)
p.55 Strawberries rotating over whipped cream: by Kseniia Konakova via Shutterstock (cropped)
p.55 Apple slices like roses pie: by Beetroot Studio via Shutterstock (cropped)
p.56 Rectangular lemon pie by Legat33 via Shutterstock (cropped)
p.56 Apple crumble pie with hearts: by Janet Faye Hastings via Shutterstock
p.56 Lemon Tart- Cropped: by Vicuschka via Shutterstock (cropped)
p.56 Three Mince Pies: by Kamira via Shutterstock
p.56 Rectangular apple pie with flower and leaf details-Cropped: by AMatveev via Shutterstock (cropped)
p.56 Small heart pies: by Kim "mini cherry pies" on creative commons via flickr
p.56 Apple tart spiral- Cropped: by forden via Shutterstock (cropped)
p.56 Cherry pie Pi- Cropped: by Oksana Mizina via Shutterstock (cropped)